Creating Cuisine

Have You Got What It Takes to Be a Chef?

by Lisa Thompson

Compass Point Books ✦ Minneapolis, Minnesota

First American edition published in 2008 by
Compass Point Books
3109 West 50th Street, #115
Minneapolis, MN 55410

Editor: Julie Gassman
Designers: Jaime Martens and Lori Bye
Creative Director: Keith Griffin
Editorial Director: Nick Healy
Managing Editor: Catherine Neitge
Content Adviser: Joseph Dufek, Executive Chef,
                Bella Italia, Cape Girardeau, Missouri

Editor's note: To best explain careers to readers, the author has
created composite characters based on extensive interviews and research.

This book was manufactured with paper containing
at least 10 percent post-consumer waste.
Printed in the United States of America.

Library of Congress Cataloging-in-Publication Data
Thompson, Lisa, 1969–
  Creating cuisine: have you got what it takes to be a chef? / by Lisa Thompson
    p. cm. — (On the job)
  Includes index.
  ISBN 978-0-7565-3625-1 (library binding)
1. Cooks—Juvenile literature. 2. Cookery—Vocational guidance—Juvenile
literature. 3. Crooked Spoon (Restaurant)—Juvenile literature. I. Title. II. Series.
  TX652.5.T53 2008
  641.5092—dc22   2007035554

Image Credits: iStock Photo/Joan Vicent Cantó Roig, cover (left); Shutterstock/
Suhendri Utet, cover (right), 14; AAP, 19. All other images are from one of the
following royalty-free sources: Big Stock Photo, Dreamstime, Istock, Photo Objects,
Photos.com, and Shutterstock. Every effort has been made to contact copyright
holders of any material reproduced in this book. Any omission will be rectified in
subsequent printings if notice is given to the publishers.

Visit Compass Point Books on the Internet at *www.compasspointbooks.com*
or e-mail your request to *custserv@compasspointbooks.com*

Table of Contents

9000983643

Busy Times at The Crooked Spoon

Preparation begins

"Where are the carrots I ordered, and the herbs? Where are those herbs? Can someone find out what's happened to our meat delivery? It should have been here by now …"

Asparagus, for one of the main dishes

It's early in the day, and the deliveries have begun to arrive. The fruit and vegetable orders are checked off. Someone is chasing down the meat order. And our seafood delivery—fresh off the boat—is expected any minute. Only the finest ingredients are acceptable in my restaurant.

The Crooked Spoon's kitchen is getting ready for lunch service. This is prep time, and the kitchen is busy but calm. Stockpots are simmering, watched over by James, my apprentice. Food is prepared and seasoned. Sauces are stirred.

We need lots of potatoes!

Preparation, preparation!

PUN FUN Chefs have the skillet takes to be good at what they do.

Yummy cheese, perfect for the platter!

Fresh scallops are tasty in pasta.

The mood changes once service begins, because people sitting down to eat don't want to wait too long for their food. If we're busy, it can quickly become a high-pressure environment, where timing is everything. Being a chef is hard work with long hours, but it is also a very rewarding career.

Today is more hectic than usual—and also more exciting! Tonight's dinner service will be special. I have been preparing for this night for weeks—writing and rewriting menus, testing and tweaking recipes, tossing around new ideas, and retrying old favorites.

A very special person will be dining in my restaurant tonight— the person who introduced me to cooking.

Chives—one of my favorite herbs!

I love to select cuts of meat from a local butcher. Only the best for my restaurant.

My Love of Cooking

When I was a boy, I was always in and out of my grandmother Nana's kitchen. I would catch the smells of what was in the oven or on the stove, and I learned to predict what delicious treats were coming my way.

Nana introduced me to the magic of food. She would make me taste her cooking with my eyes closed. Then I would try to guess the ingredients she had used. Together, we would make up recipes and experiment with different combinations of ingredients.

But there was always one dish that baffled me—a delicious dessert that remained a secret because I never unlocked the combination of flavors. It seemed like a simple dish to make, but getting the flavors to balance was not easy.

I loved experimenting and trying something new with Nana.

Nana said you are never too young to enjoy food and learn about cooking.

Nana showed me how much fun cooking could be. On the weekends, early in the mornings, we would visit the markets. We tasted and smelled foods from all over the world. For my birthday each year, Nana took me to a restaurant. I began to understand the possibilities of food and cooking, and I met people who worked with food as a career.

When I finished school, I did a four-year apprenticeship to become a chef. Then I traveled the world, working in kitchens big and small. I finally returned home and opened my own restaurant, The Crooked Spoon. The restaurant is named after the tasting spoon my Nana gave me as a boy.

Tonight Nana is my special guest, along with the rest of my family. We are celebrating her 80th birthday, and I am going to make her the secret dessert!

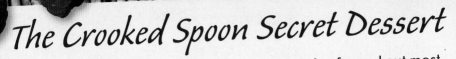

The Crooked Spoon Secret Dessert

Nana's secret recipe is a delicious berry tart. I've figured out most of the recipe, but there are a few mysteries. I wish I knew how much sugar I need. Was it 1 or 2 cups? I have to be careful that I don't get too much! The key to this dessert is to get the buttery, sweet flavor to match the tartness of the berries.

I want to add my own secret to the recipe, too. I'm going to try lining the pastry with some crushed ginger cookies. They should complement the fruit nicely.

Ingredients

Secret part A
4 cups berries (strawberries,
    blueberries, raspberries,
    and blackberries)
? cup powdered sugar
zest of 1 lemon
mascarpone cream
2 ginger cookies, crushed

Secret part B
2 1/2 cups flour
1 teaspoon salt
1 tablespoon white sugar
1 cup unsalted butter, chilled and
    cut into small pieces
? – ? cup ice water

Secret Dessert

Serves: Four

Divide pastry into four equal portions. On a lightly floured surface, roll each portion into an 8-inch circle. Place the four pastry circles into scalloped baking tins and place in the fridge for one hour. Sprinkle with a spoonful of ginger cookie crumbs. Bake pastry in a 350-degree oven for 15 minutes until golden. Cool. Spoon a layer of mascarpone into the pastry. Combine the berries and zest in a large bowl. Heap berry mixture on top of mascarpone. Lightly dust with powdered sugar and serve.

Becoming a Chef

Many chefs complete a very demanding four-year apprenticeship. Others attend culinary school. In both paths, chefs learn about and practice food preparation, cooking, and presentation. Most chefs finish their apprenticeships with a special love and passion for a particular type of cooking.

Some people say that you become a chef after completing an apprenticeship or obtaining a culinary degree. Other people say that if you prepare food in a kitchen—no matter what your position—then you are a cook.

WANTED: 1 GOOD CHEF

To be a good chef you need:

- Good health and stamina for long hours of standing

- A keen sense of smell and taste for detecting flavors and perfecting recipes

- Good coordination for working with sharp utensils

- A good memory and strong organization skills for handling all the details

- The ability to remain calm under pressure and stay focused in a busy kitchen

Keep in mind that a chef works long hours, often on weekends and holidays.

Is this for you?

Do you love food but are not sure that cooking is for you? There's a whole smorgasbord of job options that involve food. You could consider a career in restaurant management or sales for a catering company. Or you could become a restaurant consultant or a food writer or food stylist.

Food stylists prepare dishes to be photographed for cookbooks, magazines, and television.

Whichever title is used, chefs must be able to study menus and estimate the amounts of food needed, order ingredients, and prepare, season, and cook a wide variety of foods. They must be able to carve meats, prepare portions on a plate, and make sauces and garnishes. Chefs plan menus, including those for special diets, and supervise the kitchen staff. They also need to maintain strict levels of cleanliness in the kitchen.

A kitchen can be a hot, busy, and dangerous place to work.

Who's Who in The Kitchen?

Working in a kitchen is a team effort—all members have their own tasks and responsibilities. Team members must work together smoothly when a kitchen gets really busy. In a small kitchen, a team of two cooks must do everything!

Where there are several chefs working in a large kitchen, such as in a hotel, each chef will often specialize in the preparation of particular dishes or types of food.

Prep chef
A prep chef prepares food and ingredients for cooking. A prep chef does most of the chopping, peeling, cleaning, precooking, and seasoning. This saves the other cooks valuable time. In smaller kitchens, this is part of every chef's job.

Rounds cook
A rounds cook knows how to do everything. This is often considered the most challenging position in the kitchen because a rounds cook may be asked to fill any role.

Hot line cook
These cooks are in charge of the grill and hotplates. A hot line cook needs to know the best cooking temperatures for different types of meat and fish. Hot line cooks often work with the most expensive ingredients used in the restaurant. This adds to the pressure of not overcooking or burning the food.

Chefs entremetier
Prepare, cook, and present vegetables, pasta, and egg dishes.

Chefs garde manger
Prepare and present salads, cold dishes, buffets, and cold hors d'oeuvres. Hors d'oeuvres are small dishes, usually savory, served before the main meal.

Chefs saucier
Prepare, season, and cook sauces, and the meat and fish dishes they accompany. They also make soups and casseroles.

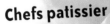

Chefs patissier
Prepare, cook, and present desserts and pastries. They may also make ice cream and sorbets.

Head chef

The head or executive chef manages the kitchen and may be responsible for more than one kitchen.

Head Chefs:
- Create new recipes and menus
- Hire staff
- Advise staff on the size of servings and standards of quality
- Check the quality of ingredients and the dishes prepared with them
- Estimate labor and food costs, and alter menus to stay within budget
- Meet with customers about menus for special occasions, such as weddings and parties
- Arrange for equipment purchases and repairs

Sous chef

Sous chef are assistants to the head chef. Sous chefs supervise specialist chefs and other kitchen workers.

Sous Chefs:
- Assist head chefs with menu planning
- Demonstrate new techniques or equipment
- Act as team leaders

Dishwasher

A dishwasher, or kitchen hand, is a general assistant in the kitchen. Dishwashers wash dishes, pots, pans, and cooking utensils. They also clean the floors, organize the storerooms, and remove the garbage. In very busy kitchens, dishwashers are invaluable because they are often the only people free to grab an ingredient or find a missing utensil. Many chefs begin their careers as dishwashers.

Kitchen items too big for the dishwasher must be washed and dried by hand.

Who's who at The Crooked Spoon?

In our medium-sized kitchen, the team consists of:

- 1 head chef (that's me)
- 2 sous chefs
- 1 chef saucier
- 2 hot line cooks
- 2 prep chef apprentices
- 1 dishwasher

A waiter must remember seating arrangements, carry dishes, answer questions about the food, and take orders.

Maître d'

A large restaurant has a maître d', which is short for maître d'hôtel, meaning "master of the house." This person takes reservations, assigns diners to tables, and manages the waiters.

Sommelier

A sommelier is a trained wine expert responsible for serving wine, as well as offering advice on specific wines and food-wine combinations.

1634
The town of Dijon in France is granted the exclusive right to make mustard.

The town of Dijon

1671
The Prince de Conde's cook kills himself by running into his sword when not enough fish is delivered for a banquet honoring King Louis XIV. The missing fish arrives 15 minutes later.

1682
Dom Perignon, a blind monk and cellarman, invents champagne at Hautevilliers Abbey, France.

Champagne, trés bonne!

1740
Paolo Adami receives a license to open the first pasta factory in Venice, Italy.

1782
The first restaurant as we know them today—with a menu, tables, waiters, and regular hours—opens in Paris. It is called the Grande Taverne de Londres.

Pasta comes in different shapes and colors.

1800
The scientist Count von Rumford develops the first commercially available kitchen stove.

1820s
Chefs begin wearing large white hats, known as toques. A cooking tradition says that a chef's toque has 100 pleats to show the number of ways an egg can be cooked.

1840
Gas stoves are first used.

1895
The Cordon Bleu, a famous French cooking school, is founded in Paris by journalist Marthe Distel to teach French cuisine to the daughters of wealthy families.

1980
Restaurant owners in Marseilles, France, agree to prepare bouillabaisse, a traditional fish stew, only from certain ingredients and using a certain method.

1993
The Food Network, a cable television network, is launched. Programming is dedicated to food and cooking.

Chefs prefer to use gas stoves because they're easier to control.

A chef's hat is properly known as a toque blanche (French for white hat).

The fish and shellfish in bouillabaisse are complemented with herbs and spices.

Famous Chefs

Marc-Antoine Careme (1784–1833)

"The king of cooks and the cook for kings."

Marc-Antoine Careme was considered the master of French cooking, creating dishes that often looked more like sculptures. He cooked for royalty and the rich and famous. His cuisine was the talk of Europe.

Via his travels, Careme introduced France to delicacies such as caviar (unfertilized fish eggs) and *paskha* (a creamy Russian cheesecake).

While in England, he produced a jellied custard set in a crown of ladyfingers (long, thin cookies). He named it the Charlotte Russe—a pastry still baked today.

Careme also prepared massive feasts. At one military festival, he served 10,000 guests from a menu that required six cows; 75 calves; 250 sheep; 8,000 turkeys; 2,000 chickens; 1,000 partridges; 500 hams; and 2,000 fish.

Careme was also a spy! He relayed information he overheard at dinner tables all over Europe back to France.

> The best caviar comes from sturgeon fish in the Caspian Sea.

PUN FUN

The chef took some cheese and made some grate things.

Family sauces

Careme classified cooking sauces into four families, each of which was based on a what is called a mother sauce:

- Allemande, based on stock with egg yolk and lemon juice, similar to hollandaise
- Béchamel, based on flour and milk
- Espagnole, based on brown stock and beef
- Velouté, based on a light broth of fish, chicken, or veal.

A later chef, Georges Auguste Escoffier, added tomato to the list of mother sauces, bringing the total to five.

Jamie Oliver (1975–)

"From quite an early age I realized the effect that good food can have on others."

Jamie Oliver is a British celebrity chef who became popular through a TV cooking show called *The Naked Chef*.

From the age of 8, Oliver started helping in the kitchen of his parents' pub, an English restaurant/bar. He had some difficulties in school because of dyslexia and left at 16 to attend a catering college. After college, he traveled to France to learn more about cooking. He was asked to make *The Naked Chef* while working in London as a sous chef.

Oliver is known for his simple recipes made from fresh ingredients. His cooking shows have been shown in 50 countries, and his cookbooks have sold millions of copies.

Oliver established the Fifteen Foundation charity in 2004 to train disadvantaged young people to work in the hospitality industry.

A World of Flavors

Every country has flavors and ingredients that make its cuisine unique. Chefs love to try foods from around the world and incorporate new ideas and flavors in their own cooking.

England—bacon, mustard, potatoes, oats, Worcestershire sauce

Ireland—cabbage, oats, oysters, potatoes

United States—corn, beans, squash, peanuts, hamburger, turkey

Mexico—chili, corn, lime, chocolate

Argentina— beef, pasta, fish, corn

Libya—lamb, lemon, coriander, onions, olive oil

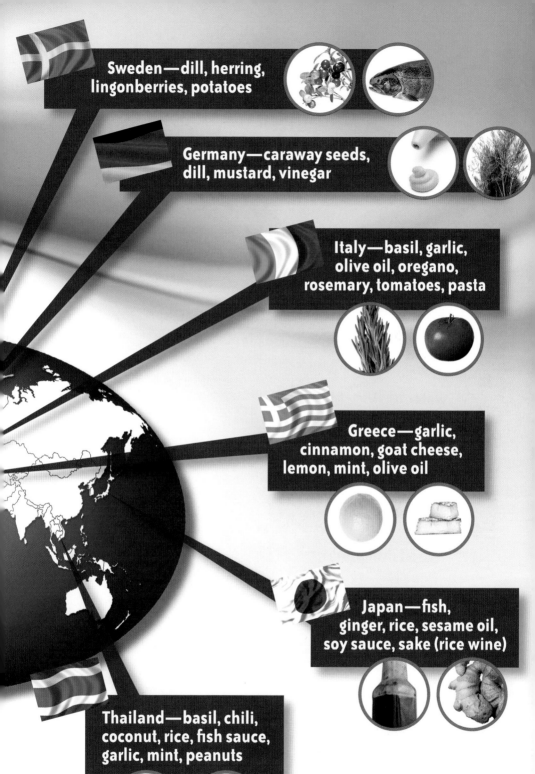

Sweden—dill, herring, lingonberries, potatoes

Germany—caraway seeds, dill, mustard, vinegar

Italy—basil, garlic, olive oil, oregano, rosemary, tomatoes, pasta

Greece—garlic, cinnamon, goat cheese, lemon, mint, olive oil

Japan—fish, ginger, rice, sesame oil, soy sauce, sake (rice wine)

Thailand—basil, chili, coconut, rice, fish sauce, garlic, mint, peanuts

Cuisine from around the world

A selection from the world's diverse food traditions

Kim chee—Korea
Fermented cabbage soaked in salt and red chili. It is usually left for several weeks before serving, but can be stored for months in clay pots buried underground.

Fugu—Japan
The meat of the poisonous puffer fish. Only specially licensed chefs are allowed to prepare fugu. Even so, several people die each year from fugu poisoning.

Water bugs—Thailand
Like giant cockroaches but with a harder shell.

Jellied cow's foot—Poland
Chopped cow's foot cooked for several hours with spices, garlic, salt, and pepper. It sits in the refrigerator with a jellylike layer of fat over the top, and is usually served with horseradish.

Blood dumplings—Sweden
Flour, reindeer blood, and salt dumplings, served with bacon, butter, and lingonberry jam.

Seal flipper pie—Canada
Fresh seal flippers, pork fat, onions, and Worcestershire sauce, baked in a pastry-covered pie.

Feeling REALLY hungry?

For possibly the largest dish on any menu, try whole roasted camel, sometimes served at Bedouin wedding feasts in the Middle East. It's a roast camel stuffed with a sheep's carcass, which is stuffed with a chicken, which is stuffed with a fish, which is stuffed with eggs. Any gaps are stuffed with rice and nuts.

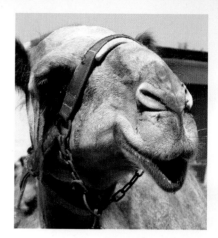

Other specials currently not on our menu

Tripe, made from the stomach lining of cows or sheep.

Black pudding and apples. Blood is the main ingredient in black pudding.

Snails

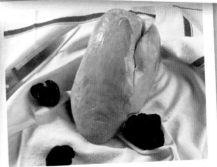

Fois gras (fattened liver of a duck or goose) and truffles (a fungus).

Chef Sense: Tongue and Nose

Tongue tasting

The most important muscle for a chef to train is the tongue. The tongue has different types of nerve endings called taste buds that detect the four basic flavors—sour, salty, bitter, and sweet.

bitter sour

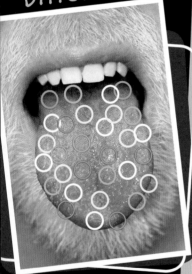

salty sweet

People once thought that certain areas of the tongue detected certain tastes—sour tastes on the sides, sweet tastes at the front, bitter tastes at the back, and salty tastes detected all over the tongue. Now it is known that there are only small differences in sensitivity across the tongue, and sweet, sour, salty, and bitter are tasted all over the tongue.

There can be large differences in our ability to taste. People with a very sensitive sense of taste are called super tasters— they find vegetables bitter, particularly brussel sprouts.

Being nosey

Your nose lets you know the differences among burned toast, roast lamb, and chocolate cake. It does this with help from body parts deep inside your nasal cavity and head. On the roof of the nasal cavity (the space behind your nose) is the olfactory epithelium. This tissue contains receptors sensitive to odor molecules. The receptors are very small. There are at least 10 million of them in your nose!

There are hundreds of types of odor receptors, each with the ability to sense certain molecules. When the odor receptors are stimulated, signals travel along the olfactory nerve to the brain. The brain interprets the combination of odor molecules to recognize any one of about 10,000 different smells.

Nothing smells as good as freshly baked bread!

Test your nosey food critic

The ability to smell and taste go together, because odors from foods allow us to taste more fully. Try this simple experiment. Take a bite of any food and think about how it tastes. Then pinch and hold your nose and take another bite. Notice the difference?

To Your Stations

All kitchens—no matter how large or small—can be divided into five basic areas: storage, preparation, cooking, washing, and serving.

A kitchen is designed like a factory. Raw materials (ingredients) come in at one end of the production line and exit at the other end as a meal ready to be served.

Kitchens are divided into clearly defined areas, called stations, that handle different tasks. Because a kitchen is a busy and sometimes dangerous environment, it is organized to make it easy to work in and move around. For example, waiters and kitchen staff meet where dishes are served and dirty plates collect, but otherwise keep out of each other's way.

shelves for storage

access to dining room

microwave oven

stove top and grill

Just like home?

Although a commercial kitchen in a restaurant has the same purpose as your kitchen at home, most things in a commercial kitchen are bigger. While you may have a dishwasher at home, a commercial kitchen might have two or three. Rather than just a fridge, a commercial kitchen might have a walk-in cool room. A commercial kitchen usually has more than one oven, and large, heavy-duty stoves. A restaurant kitchen also has strong exhaust fans for removing hot air from the kitchen.

exhaust fan

ladles

countertops for food preparation

chopping boards

oven

Carving up the Kitchen

Every chef has a set of knives. Although there are many types of knives, a chef's set usually includes:

- **Chef's (or French) knife:** Used to chop, slice, and mince meat, fruits, and vegetables
- **Cleaver:** Used to chop large pieces of meat, often cutting through bones
- **Carving knife:** Used to carve large cuts of meat into serving-sized pieces
- **Filleting knife:** Used to remove bones from fish
- **Boning knife:** Used to separate raw meat from bone
- **Paring knife:** Used to peel, slice, trim, and dice small fruits, vegetables, and cheese
- **Bread knife:** Used to slice bread and cakes
- **Sharpening stone and steel:** Used to sharpen and realign a knife's edge

A knife block protects blades when not in use.

Depending on a chef's area of expertise, he or she may use special preparation tools. Here are just a few possibilities:

- Whisk for whipping together ingredients such as eggs, cream, and milk
- Vegetable peeler for removing the peel of thin-skinned vegetables such as carrots; also used to make garnishes
- Mortar and pestle for grinding spices and herbs together
- Molds and piping bags for decorative details on desserts

Different nozzles for the piping bag produce different decorative patterns.

Preparing salmon in a Japanese restaurant.

Sushi slicers

Sushi is a Japanese dish traditionally made with rice and either vegetables or seafood, with egg occasionally added. Raw fish is a key ingredient.

Sushi chefs use special knives to prepare their dishes, including knives designed to cut particular species of fish. For example, the fugu *hiki* is specifically designed to fillet the puffer fish (fugu), and the *unagisaki hocho* is designed for filleting eel. For preparing very large fish, such as large tuna, a knife more than 3 feet long may be used.

Unlike most knives, sushi knives are sharpened on only one edge. So there are different knives for right-handed and left-handed chefs!

Sushi

Whisk

Pizza cutter

Vegetable peeler

Grater

Juicer

Mortar and pestle

Ladle

29

Measuring Up

Cooking has its own measuring system—based on spoons and cups—that is different from the metric and standard measuring systems. But even these measures change depending on what country you are cooking in!

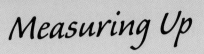

Measuring cup

Basic measurements a chef must know:

1 teaspoon (t or tsp.) = 5 milliliters
1 tablespoon (T or tbsp.) = 3 teaspoons = 15 milliliters
1 cup (c) = 250 milliliters
2 cups = 500 milliliters
4 cups = 1 liter

Measuring spoons

Kitchen scale

Kitchen timer

Heaped or even?

In their recipes, chefs sometimes include extra instructions for measuring the correct amount of an ingredient. Here's how to measure out what the chef wants:

Firmly packed: Press the ingredient tightly into the measuring device

Lightly packed: Press the ingredient lightly into the measuring device

Even or level: Level the top of the ingredient with a spatula or knife, so that it is even with the rim

Rounded: Allow the ingredient to pile up above the rim of the measuring device

Heaping or heaped: Measure as much of the ingredient as the measuring device will hold

Preheat the oven to avoid burning your hard work!

Leveling off the flour

Feeling REALLY hungry?

As an oven heats, it puts out extra heat to reach the selected temperature. If you put food in the oven before it has reached the desired temperature, it could burn. Preheating an oven usually takes five to 10 minutes.

Cooking 101

It is part of a chef's job to unlock the wonderful secrets that food holds—how certain ingredients taste when combined with others, how foods react to different kinds of cooking, and how ingredients can be treated and prepared. Great chefs are always pushing the boundaries of what food can taste and look like.

PUN FUN
When the Italian chef became angry, he gave everyone a pizza his mind.

Basic methods of cooking

- **Baking:** Cooking by dry heat in the oven

- **Roasting:** Cooking by high-heat baking (usually with some fat added)

- **Broiling:** Cooking at a high temperature with an overhead heat source

- **Grilling:** Cooking over an open heat element

- **Frying:** Cooking in a pan with a moderate amount of fat at a moderate temperature, or deep-frying while submerged in oil at a high temperature

- **Boiling:** Cooking in boiling liquid

Sautéed mushrooms

Soft boiled eggs

Most chefs cannot work without butter and oil, garlic, salt, and herbs.

STOCK UP

Possibly a chef's best friend is stock—the liquid in which meat, fish, or vegetables are simmered for long periods. A stock is the basis of most sauces and soups.

Asian dishes are often cooked using bamboo steamers.

- **Simmering:** Cooking in liquid below boiling point

- **Sautéing:** Cooking in a pan quickly in a small amount of fat at a high temperature

- **Steaming:** Cooking food by exposing it directly to steam

- **Braising:** Browning food in a little fat, then slowly cooking in a covered pot with a little liquid at a low temperature

Steamed dumplings

33

Works of Art

Good cooking tastes great—
and it looks great. Part of the
enjoyment of eating a meal
prepared by a chef is the way
the food is presented.

How would you present
a cooked whole fish? With or
without the eyes? How would you include a mushroom
sauce with a steak dish? Poured over the meat or next to it on
the plate? The presentation of a dish is one way that chefs add
personal style to their work and create culinary works of art.

A garnish is a decoration that adds to
the presentation of a dish. A simple rule
of garnishing is to use ingredients in the
dish itself to decorate the plate. This is the
easiest and most sensible way to garnish,
because you know the tastes will blend.

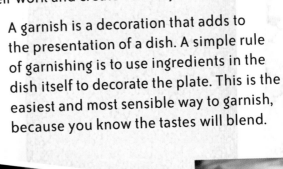

Plate up

The way a dish is assembled on a plate is called plating. Here are the golden rules of plating that every chef remembers:

- Don't overcrowd a plate with food. Leave one-third (or sometimes two-thirds) of the plate empty.

- Odd numbers of food items on a plate generally look better than even numbers.

- Put food on the plate—no matter what its temperature—immediately before serving it.

- If serving hot food, make sure that the food and the plate are hot when plating.

- Make sure plate edges are clean. If you need to clean them, use a moist paper towel in one circular sweep.

Easy garnish ideas
- Chives on a veggie-filled omelet
- A splash of cream drizzled over a thick soup
- Ground salt sprinkled on a steak
- A bed of shredded carrots under deviled eggs

35

Signature Dishes

Some dishes have become so popular that they are made over and over again. A famous dish that identifies a chef is known as a signature dish.

Peach Melba

This dessert was created for an Australian opera singer, Dame Nellie Melba, by the great French chef Auguste Escoffier in 1893. Kaiser Wilhelm II once told Escoffier, "I am the emperor of Germany, but you are the emperor of chefs."

2 cups fresh peaches, peeled and sliced
2 cups raspberries, fresh or frozen
¾ cup sugar
2 tablespoons water
vanilla ice cream

In a saucepan, bring peaches, raspberries, sugar, and water to a boil. Reduce heat and simmer for five minutes. Chill, if desired, and serve with ice cream. Serves eight people.

Waldorf Salad

A salad created by Oscar Tschirky—known as Oscar of the Waldorf—for the opening of the Waldorf-Astoria Hotel in New York in 1893. (Tschirky didn't include any nuts in the original, though.)

3 cups diced Red Delicious apples
½ cup diced celery
¼ cup walnut pieces
⅓ cup mayonnaise
1 tablespoon lemon juice

Toss apples with lemon juice. Add remaining ingredients and mix well. Serves four people.

Sachertorte

Possibly the world's most famous chocolate cake, invented by a 16-year-old apprentice cook, Franz Sacher, in 1832 in Vienna, Austria. The original recipe is a well-kept secret.

½ cup butter
½ cup powdered sugar
6 egg yolks
4.5 ounces chocolate, melted
½ cup, plus 1 tablespoon flour
6 egg whites
½ cup fine granulated sugar
apricot jam

Beat together the butter and powdered sugar. Gradually add in the egg yolks and the melted chocolate, stirring constantly. Beat the egg whites with the granulated sugar to stiff peaks, and mix them into the chocolate batter. Gently fold in the flour.

Place the mixture in a buttered 9-inch spring form pan and bake for 60 minutes at 350° F. Let cool, remove from the mold, slice through the middle horizontally, and fill with a layer of apricot jam. Glaze with chocolate. Serves eight people.

All in a Day's Work at The Crooked Spoon

I wake up thinking about the specials we can prepare for lunch and dinner at The Crooked Spoon. To keep the menu fresh, specials are new dishes that are created from produce that is in season.

Shallots for cooking, radishes for a special sauce

10 A.M.—I arrive at the restaurant and check the deliveries for quality and accuracy. I ensure we received what we ordered. Matthew, one of my prep chefs, is already storing the deliveries.

I make sure the kitchen was cleaned thoroughly after last night's work. This lets me know that my staffers are keeping up with their responsibilities.

10:30 A.M.—I check that the cool rooms and storerooms are tidy and that stock levels are sufficient. I look at the reservations list for lunch and dinner to get a feel for how busy the day will be.

Time to get started!

10:45 A.M.—The other chefs begin to arrive. I run through the menu with the sous chefs and discuss the specials that I have in mind. I ask Fiona, one of the sous chefs, to suggest and prepare specials for tomorrow's dinner menu. She will present them for tasting by the staff tomorrow afternoon.

Chop, chop, so much to cut!

11 A.M.—The chefs prepare their stations—their work areas—and begin seasoning, chopping, and saucing.

Sautéed pork for the salad

12 noon—The Crooked Spoon is now open for lunch! When the first order is taken—for the Warm Pork and Asparagus Spinach Salad—I call it out loudly. Calling the orders sounds chaotic when the kitchen is really busy, but it keeps the staff focused so they can concentrate on cooking, presentation, and timing.

Before every dish leaves the kitchen, I check that the presentation meets my standards, and that it was prepared in a reasonable amount of time. I don't want my customers to wait too long for their meals!

Asparagus spears—yummy!

3 P.M.—The kitchen closes after lunch and everything is cleaned and packed away. Food stocks are checked and new orders phoned to suppliers.

Fresh, crusty loaves—smell good!

The staff takes a well-deserved break before The Crooked Spoon reopens for dinner, and my special guest arrives.

We make and bake our own bread.

4:30 P.M.—While the staff members are on their break, I work on my special dessert for Nana tonight. The berries are wonderfully juicy and fresh, but I must get their sweetness to balance with the pastry.

Look at the beautiful berries— it's going to be great!

5 P.M.—The staff returns, and we prepare for the dinner service.

We all sit down to taste samples of the specials and run through the ingredients. Our customers are sure to ask questions about what is in the dishes and how they are prepared. I give everyone a quick taste of my special dessert. They are wide-eyed with delight!

The pastry cup, ready for the fruit mixture

6 P.M.—The Crooked Spoon opens again, and diners begin to arrive. We're ready and waiting for the first order.

6:15 P.M.—The first order is in. I begin delegating tasks to the various chefs and sections. The cooking is under way.

7 P.M.—Peering through the kitchen door window, I see my family arrive with Nana. What will she order?

It's getting busy now.

Cut quickly, but be careful!

7:20 P.M.—The order from Nana's table reaches the kitchen. She has ordered a beetroot and herb risotto as a first course, followed by the pan-fried rabbit and warm apple salad. Great choice! I choose to cook Nana's main dish myself.

Pasta on the boil

7:25 P.M.—Suddenly there is a loud crash from the cool room. A container of broccoli has fallen onto some pastry cups that were ready for one of the dessert dishes. There is no time to make more pastry cups, so that dish will have to come off the menu.

The kitchen is getting busier and hotter as the oven and hot plates swing into action.

Got to peel the prawns quickly!

Even though it's frantic, you have to stay in control.

The kitchen heats up!

41

7:50 P.M.—One of the waiters tells me that he has lost an order, and a couple has been waiting for 40 minutes for their meals. I am not happy! Producing these dishes becomes my first priority.

I entrust my best sous chef with completing Nana's dishes.

8 P.M.—The kitchen is hot, alive, and buzzing with activity. Orders are called out. "Another chicken, three beef, a pasta on 12." Side dishes are called for. Sauces are poured. Garnish containers need to be restocked. Pots and pans are being shuffled over flames, and from front burners to back burners. Every station is a flurry of activity and a blur of hands.

The stove's on fire tonight!

Have to cook the same thing three times.

Roast beef—medium

9:10 P.M.—The pace is slowing now, and I switch my attention to Nana's dessert. She hasn't ordered a dessert, so my creation will be a surprise. I've decided to keep its presentation very simple, positioned alone on a simple white plate. I watch nervously as the waiter weaves out through the dining room to Nana's table with the dessert.

Roasted peppers—fresh from the oven

Peering through the kitchen door, I see the look of surprise and (I hope!) delight on her face. She gathers a spoonful of dessert to her lips and closes her eyes.

I hold my breath. Then Nana cries aloud toward the kitchen, "Bravo, my boy. You've done it! You have unlocked the tastes in our special dessert, and it is DELICIOUS."

Icing a cake — steady hands required.

The other diners in the restaurant begin to look back and forth between Nana and the kitchen. And then we are bombarded with orders for The Crooked Spoon Secret Dessert!

It is going to be a long, hot, and happy night in the kitchen.

Happy birthday, Nana.

Nana's secret dessert

43

Follow These Steps to Become a Chef

Finish high school with the best grades you can get, especially in any hospitality or food technology subjects offered at your school.

Work as a kitchen hand, even part time, because it will give you invaluable experience in a commercial kitchen. Cooking is one of the few occupations where you can get most of your training on the job.

Complete an apprenticeship or degree in the hospitality industry, as a general chef or a specialized pastry or baking chef. An apprenticeship combines practical, paid work with structured training to give you both experience and a qualification. When approaching employers about an apprenticeship, ask plenty of questions about whether you will get the practical experience and full range of opportunities that you are after.

Learn about the industry you have joined and its opportunities. Start networking and building contacts as early as possible.

Be prepared to work long hours, especially early in your career. Most cooks work shifts, including weekends and holidays. This could include split shifts, which means taking the afternoon off between lunch and dinner.

Step 6

Take a course on running a small business if you want to set up your own restaurant, café, or catering business.

Step 7

Never stop learning! The secret to being a successful chef is always wanting to touch, taste, and learn about food. The more you explore the world of food, the more confident you will become.

Courses to study in school

- Consumer science courses that emphasize cooking or nutrition
- Business math
- Business administration
- Community education cooking classes

Opportunities for chefs

- No chef can ever learn all there is to know about food. There are endless opportunities to grow as a professional, new cuisines to master, new dishes to create.

- In the hospitality industry, there is always the opportunity to work in another country. This is all part of widening your experience of various ingredients and styles of cooking.

- You could start your own business—a restaurant, café, or catering company.

- Your skills as a chef could be used in accommodation services (hotels, motels, bed-and-breakfasts), food and beverage businesses (cafés, restaurants), tourism-related services (cooking for airlines and cruise ships), and the conference and events industries.

- You may choose to specialize in a particular type of cuisine, such as seafood, vegetarian, or French cuisine.

45

Find Out More

In the Know

- Experts say there will be plenty of job openings for chefs through 2014. However, competition in the top kitchens of high-end restaurants will be steep.

- More and more chefs are working in prepared foods sections of grocery or specialty food stores. The meals-to-go that are sold in these areas are in high demand with consumers.

- The District of Columbia, New Jersey, and New York are the top paying areas for chefs in the United States.

- Average annual earnings for chefs and head cooks in 2006 was $37,880. The lowest 10 percent earned $20,160, and the highest 10 percent earned $60,730.

Further Reading

D'Amico, Joan, and Karen Eich Drummond. *The Coming to America Cookbook: Delicious Recipes and Fascinating Stories from America's Many Cultures*. Hoboken, N.J.: Wiley, 2005.

Hinton, Kerry. *Cool Careers Without College for People Who Love Food*. New York: Rosen Publishing Group, 2004.

Locricchio, Matthew. *The International Cookbook for Kids*. Tarrytown, N.Y.: Marshall Cavendish Corp., 2004.

Maze, Stephanie. *I Want to Be a Chef*. San Diego: Harcourt Brace, 1999.

On the Web

For more information on this topic, use FactHound.

1. Go to *www.facthound.com*

2. Type in this book ID: 0756536251

3. Click on the *Fetch It* button.

Glossary

apprentice—a person who works for and learns from a skilled professional for a set amount of time; this time period is known as the apprenticeship

broth—thin soup of meat, fish, or vegetable stock

buffet—meal of several dishes where guests help themselves

catering—to provide and sometimes serve food

commercial kitchen—kitchen that prepares food for sale

cool room—a room that serves as a freezer or chilling space for a commercial kitchen

course—a part of a meal served alone

cuisine—style of cooking

culinary—related to cooking or the kitchen

food technology—study of food production, handling, and storage

garnish—something added to a dish for flavor or decoration

glaze—to make a surface shiny by putting a liquid substance (a glaze) onto it and leaving it or heating it until it dries

hospitality industry—industry that provides accommodations, food, and beverages; includes restaurants, bars, hotels, resorts, and travel and tourism companies

hygiene—degree to which people keep themselves or their surroundings clean, especially to prevent disease

plating—act of arranging food on a plate

preheating—to heat an oven to a particular temperature before putting food in it

recipe—set of instructions telling you how to prepare food, including a list of what ingredients are needed

special—dish that is available in a restaurant on a particular day

station—area where a person is assigned to work

stock—liquid in which meat, fish, or vegetables are simmered for long periods; also refers to supplies

zest—the thin outer peel of a citrus fruit used for flavoring

Index

Look for More Books in This Series:

Art in Action: Have You Got What It Takes to Be an Animator?

Battling Blazes: Have You Got What It Takes to Be a Firefighter?

Cordially Invited: Have You Got What It Takes to Be an Event Planner?

Focusing on Fitness: Have You Got What It Takes to Be a Personal Trainer?

Hard Hat Area: Have You Got What It Takes to Be a Contractor?

Pop the Hood: Have You Got What It Takes to Be an Auto Technician?

Sea Life Scientist: Have You Got What It Takes to Be a Marine Biologist?

Trendsetter: Have You Got What It Takes to Be a Fashion Designer?

Wild About Wildlife: Have You Got What It Takes to Be a Zookeeper?